THE 7 FRIENDSHIP CYCLES

The Secret to a Happy Friendship

Tina Luckett

Lucketteer LLC.
Van Buren Twp, MI

The 7 Friendship Cycles © Copyright 2023 Tina Luckett

All rights reserved. No part of this publication may be reproduced, distributed, or transmitted in any form or by any means, including photocopying, recording, or other electronic or mechanical methods, without the prior written permission of the publisher, except in the case of brief quotations embodied in critical reviews and certain other noncommercial uses permitted by copyright law.

The resources in this book are provided for informational purposes only and should not be used to replace the specialized training and professional judgment of a health care or mental health care professional. Neither the author nor the publisher can be held responsible for the use of the information provided within this book. Please always consult a trained professional before making any decision regarding the treatment of yourself or others.

This is a work of non-fiction. Names, characters, places, and incidents are either the product of the author's imagination or are used fictitiously. Any resemblance to actual persons, living or dead, businesses, companies, events, or locales is entirely coincidental. Any perceived slight of any individual or organization is purely unintentional. To protect the privacy of others, certain names have been changed.

Library of Congress Control Number: 2020925808

Publisher's Cataloging-in-Publication data
Names: Luckett, Tina, author. | Johnson Lewis, Lisha, audiobook narrator. Title: The 7 friendship cycles: the secret to a happy friendship / Tina Luckett; audiobook narrated by Lisha Johnson Lewis.
Description: Includes bibliographical references. | Van Buren Township, MI: Lucketteer, LLC, 2023.
Identifiers: LCCN 2020925808 | ISBN: 978-1-7364090-7-7 (paperback) | 978-1-7364090-9-1 (ebook) | 978-1-7364090-8-4 (audio)
Subjects: LCSH Friendship. | Female friendship. | Women—Psychology. |Interpersonal relations. | Self-help. | BISAC FAMILY & RELATIONSHIPS / Friendship | BODY, MIND & SPIRIT / Inspiration & Personal Growth | SELF-HELP / Personal Growth / General
Classification: LCC BF575.F66 .L93 2023 | DDC 158.2/5/082—dc23

For more information, email tinaluckett7@gmail.com or visit website: www.tinaluckett.com

Edited by: McKinley, Nicole, Keely Catarineau, Becky HTE at Hot Tree Editing, Graeme Hague and Stephanie Parent at Polgarus Studio, Michelle Williams at Fiverr, Iantha Ussin (Chapters 1-3)

Beta Readers: Donna Lehman, India Smiley, Terri Hart, Linda Jackson, Paula Wheeler, Dorothy Williamson

Cover design: Designs for Writers

Formatting: Polgarus Studio

Writing Course: Self Publishing Formula, Mark Dawson, and James Blatch

Writing Coach: Ramy Vance, aka R.E. Vance, Self-Publishing School

Author photo: Murtaza Bikanerwala, Seattle, WA

Dedication

To the two ladies dearest to my heart, my amazing daughters:
Breanna Luckett Jackson and Areanna Luckett
May you continue to make me smile. I'm so proud of you both!

*"There is no distance too far between friends,
for friendship gives wings to the heart."*
~ Kathy Kay Benudiz

Contents

Introduction: What I Know for Sure 1
Growing Apart 3
What is Friendship? 7
The Conflict 11

Part 1 – Reason (Friendship Develops) 17
    FRIENDSHIP CYCLE #1: The Seed 19
    FRIENDSHIP CYCLE #2: The Bark 31

Part 2 – Season (Friendship Choices) 39
    FRIENDSHIP CYCLE #3: The Branch 41
    FRIENDSHIP CYCLE #4: The Vine 51

Part 3 – Lifetime (Friendship Goals) 57
    FRIENDSHIP CYCLE #5: The Leaf 59
    FRIENDSHIP CYCLE #6: The Root 67
    FRIENDSHIP CYCLE #7: The Trunk 77

Practical Ways to Deepen Your Friendships 81
A Final Word 85
Acknowledgments 87
Q&A with the Author 89
Sources 91
The 7 Friendship Cycles Profile Quiz 95

Also available from Tina Luckett:
The Boss Moves Series:

Foreword

For as long as I can remember, authentic friendships have been vital to me while journeying through life. As a young adult, I watched the author host numerous holiday dinners, inviting friends, family members, and neighbors for a seat at the table and asking for nothing in return. I admired from a distance how she treasured friendships. People would travel in from out of state just to attend the Lucketts' holiday dinners.

Using a tree as a metaphor, *The 7 Friendship Cycles* is a manual that provides adequate information and instruction on how to matriculate through the various cycles of friendship. We don't always realize the impact others have on us and how genuine friendships go through life cycles like a tree. The author not only defines various types of friends, but she also incorporates her own personal experiences of gains and losses amongst friends.

Friends are like plants; some do not require as much water as others. Know when to stop pouring! – Dr. India C. Smiley, Author of *Wonder Woman, Where Are You?*

Introduction:
What I Know for Sure

The key to understanding lasting friendships can be found in the elements of a growing tree.

I have been envisioning this concept for decades while observing, learning, and meditating on how best to translate my knowledge and experiences into a book that I believe will forever change lives and notions about friendship. I believe God put this book on my heart for a reason, and it has taken me over twenty years to understand all of His visions for me to get it right. The final push was an intervention by my daughters and their encouragement to start writing everything down because they understood that *writing the vision turns it into a reality*.

In *The 7 Friendship Cycles*, I use the elements of a tree to explain how women can create, nurture, and maintain healthy relationships. These cycles will shine a light on how you and your friends view each other. When you can identify the type of friend you are, you will have a better understanding of yourself and your friendships. As we all know, building and keeping friendships is incredibly challenging and demands a lot of time. One of the reasons for this is that we all come from different backgrounds and have different perspectives on life in general. When these differing factors meet, reaching a point of agreement is not always easy.

We must understand that we need friends to maintain a healthy and positive lifestyle. A life without friends may seem like a never-ending struggle filled with heartache and isolation. However, with the right tools, resources, and patience, a potential friend can become a great one. God places friends in our lives for a purpose; they come to us for a reason, a season, or a lifetime. Once you realize their purpose, you can flourish and expand your horizons together.

Without these important relationships, many women feel alone as they navigate the obstacles in their daily lives, but it doesn't have to be that way. One important thing to consider is how we use the title "friend" because it is often used too loosely. For the word "friend" to hold any power, it must be earned, as having the right friends around you is the key to a successful life full of happiness. For instance, on social media, everyone is labeled our "friend" when, in actuality, most are strangers looking for other people to validate them. We should label people according to their role: acquaintance, associate, colleague, potential friend, and even a stranger.

On the last pages of this book, you will find the quiz I created called "The 7 Friendship Cycles Profile." The profile will help you evaluate and determine the purpose of your current friendships. After reading this book, you will look at your friends differently. Each friendship cycle has its own potential for growth, and sustaining and maintaining harmony will be the glue that holds the friendship together.

As you proceed through the friendship cycles, remember a friendship that starts as a small seed can eventually blossom into an everlasting forest.

Growing Apart

On one of my trips to visit my father on the Amtrak train from Ann Arbor, Michigan, to Milwaukee, Wisconsin, a woman in the seat across from me leaned over and introduced herself.

"Hi, my name is Connie. May I inquire about what you are working on?" She looked at the papers on the seat next to me.

I replied, "Well, I'm writing a communication book about friendships. I came up with this concept that all people go through seven friendship cycles."

"Wahoo! That's interesting. I happen to be on my way to see a good friend of mine. I've been invited to attend her reveal party for her unborn child. Can I ask your opinion? Maybe you can tell me if it's all right for me to feel guilty or not."

Connie had a nervous look in her eyes.

"Sure," I said.

"I have been friends with Donna since elementary school, and we kept in touch throughout college. Donna married a guy named Bobby, who she met her first year away from home."

"Do you like him?" I asked.

"I didn't at first because I didn't think he was mature enough for her, but it has been twenty years now, and they're still happily married." She continued, "They are expecting their fourth child in a couple of months, and I'm happy for them."

"So, what's your question?"

"Here's the deal: we have always been close, but now we're not.

So, my question is, why do friends grow apart? She is married, a mother, and living in the suburbs, and I'm single and concentrating on my career. I get that our lives are very different, but I miss the closeness we once shared. I told her that I miss chatting with her every day."

"What did she say when you told her how you felt?"

"Donna mentioned not having much time for social stuff anymore, with her responsibilities and work schedule taking up much of her time. I feel like I'm always there for her, but she is never there for me. For instance, she invites me to all her events, which I have always attended, but she has never visited me in Florida. I'm at a point where I'm rethinking our friendship, and I'm feeling guilty about it. I don't want to lose her as a friend, but we don't have much in common anymore. Am I wrong to feel this way?"

"No, you're not," I replied.

According to Dr. Suzanne Degges-White, friendships involve two key dimensions: interdependence and voluntary participation. Friendship is a complex process that requires each party's desire to engage and connect with the other, share in one another's experiences and thoughts, and establish a sense of belongingness. To grow and maintain a successful friendship, the members must show admiration, respect, trust, and genuine concern for each other's interests and offer emotional and instrumental support.

Connie's experience with her friend Donna is a very common one. After researching friendships for decades and earning my Master of Science degree in Leadership, my conclusion regarding why friends grow apart is the *lack of communication*. Connie wants to feel like their relationship is still adding value. She wants to feel connected, accepted, and valued by Donna. It is not wrong for her to have these feelings. Connie and Donna are failing by not communicating their feelings to each other.

On the other hand, Donna has a valid point; she doesn't have much time to hang out or chat. Donna needs to explain to Connie, who doesn't have the same lifestyle and may not fully understand her point of view, how being a mom and wife sucks up all her free time.

In cases like this, simple communication could resolve the problem completely. If the two ladies keep their communication lines open and maintain an understanding, it will prevent them from feeling like the friendship has ended.

SAP TIME
(Your Thoughts)

Which of your friends have you drifted away from?

_____

_____

_____

_____

_____

_____

_____

_____

_____

_____

What is Friendship?

Merriam-Webster's Dictionary defines friendship as "a relationship between friends." To me, friendship is a committed relationship between two people who share an emotional bond. They care deeply, love one another, and share similar interests, feelings, and ideas. Friendship is our lifeline, our journey to happiness.

Without a doubt, friendship is the most precious gift you can freely give anyone and the most significant tie someone may wish for in their life. Lucky ones are those who have friends they can trust and count on in any given situation. Unlucky ones are those who tried but weren't successful just yet.

You will meet many friends in your life, but only a few of them stick with you until the end. True friends stick by your side through good and bad times. When our friendships are going well, we are happy and healthy and want the world to know about it. But when they're not, our health starts to decline, and life as we know it becomes one big blob of bad outcomes.

It's important to get a basic working knowledge of how friendships develop. Good friendships don't just "happen," and they can't be forced to develop quickly. All relationships progress through stages, and in the process, they show up naturally over time, often while you're unaware of what's going on. According to Erica Djossa from The Love Compass, "Looking at the different stages of friendships in our lives allows us to view the stages objectively and become aware of the process/time it takes to develop a close friendship with another person."

The stages of friendship are acquaintance, peer friend, close friend, and best friend. Let's take a closer look at each one:

STAGES OF FRIENDSHIP:

- **Acquaintance:** All friendships initially start out as an acquaintance. This is someone with whom you share and know "public" information (facts) about. You may interact with them but don't consider them your friend. It takes just a few times seeing someone to consider them an acquaintance, but that person may or may not move past this stage or level of friendship.

- **Peer Friend:** This is someone with whom you discover common interests, activities, and concerns. You may learn a little about each other's goals, wishes, or opinions. It takes some time to develop the status of a peer because it implies that you have encountered the person on numerous occasions and have some type of regular involvement with them.

- **Close Friend:** A close friend is someone you consider part of your inner circle and with whom you share similar life goals and values. These people know the most about your life and have likely been through a few ups and downs with you. Close friends are generally those you see and talk to the most.

- **Best Friend:** A best friend is someone with whom you have built a strong trust and could share almost everything with. The development of a best friend relationship takes time and experience together; it cannot happen overnight. It implies a commitment to support one another and requires both parties' honesty, loyalty, and discretion.

THE 7 FRIENDSHIP CYCLES

I have discussed the four stages of friendships; now, let's review the three types of friendships.

In his *Nicomachean Ethics*, Aristotle argues that friendships are initiated to improve our lives and therefore involve good actions that concern the well-being of the parties involved. Aristotle also described three types of friendships—utility, pleasure, and virtue:

- **Friendship of Utility** is a relationship people get into mainly due to the benefits of each other. In this type of friendship, one gets involved with someone who is useful to them in some way. The aim of the developed friendship is always to benefit from each other, and if such benefits no longer exist nor are realized, then the friendship may not be necessary and, as a result, may be dissolved.

- **Friendships of Pleasure** occur between those who enjoy each other's company and are mostly driven by emotions. The main aim of this type of friendship is to provide enjoyment and pleasure to members. People remain friends and committed to the inclination of the moment as long as they continue to obtain pleasure from the friendships. These relationships can, however, be broken when friends' tastes change, and they no longer derive satisfaction and positive emotions from such affiliations.

- **Virtue Friendships** are the most powerful, enduring, and based on mutual respect and admiration. Aristotle argues that virtue friendships are the best as members derive both benefits and pleasure from such relationships. Virtue friendships are long-term and normally arise from those who have shared values and goals and want the best for each other.

The Conflict

The idea that women cannot get along with each other has become one of the most common and widely agreed upon notions about the female gender. When I asked people why this is, I received many answers, ranging from women being: jealous, envious, hateful, competitive, lacking trust, and willing to betray each other. One way or the other, negativity was the underlying condition for each reason.

Dr. Iyanla Vanzant, an American inspirational speaker specializing in personal development and spiritual evolution, reflected on why women can't get along on her hit television show, *Iyanla: Fix My Life*. "Women can't get along because we are afraid. We are afraid to be vulnerable, we are afraid to be soft, we are afraid to be hurt, and most of all we are afraid of our power. So, we become controlled, aggressive, and violent because no one taught us how not to be. Why can't women get along? Because we have been taught that it is better to be bad than to be powerful."

So, the question is, when will women stop being "bad" and become "powerful"?

FATHER-DAUGHTER RELATIONSHIP

The men in our lives play a part in the women's inability to get along. Take a moment to digest that. A father's relationship with his daughter is very crucial because some girls might pick up bad habits as a child and carry them into adulthood. These bad habits could harm a girl's friendships later in life.

Research from *Psychology Today* states, "Dad creates a daughter's conscious and unconscious relationship expectations. If there was a dad or other male caregiver in your early life, he probably set the first model of how a relationship with a man would be." This makes a lot of sense since girls tend to look up to the males in their lives. I believe dads unknowingly show their daughters how to compete.

When I was a child growing up in Milwaukee, Wisconsin, with my dad, his common-law wife, two brothers, and four sisters, I remember my dad being extremely strict with us girls. He was not so strict with the boys. They could get away with a lot of stuff. For instance, my brothers could have girlfriends, but I would've been in so much trouble if my dad knew I liked one of the neighborhood boys. I always felt like I was one of my dad's "favorite children," and I tried extremely hard to stay in that position. Sometimes, I would get in trouble because I would start a fight with my sisters. I got punished for a week when I got caught, but I didn't care. I wanted his attention, so being stuck in my room for the week was worth it.

Fighting was my way of keeping my sisters under my control. Looking back on it as an adult, I know now that wasn't smart on my part. I learned that this is where jealousy and envy crept in. While wanting my dad's approval, I would pit the family against each other, which caused a lot of hateful behavior between my sisters and me. As we grew older, it was a never-ending cycle of fights, miscommunication, and quarrels. This created the need for us to compare, compete, and communicate in negative ways. We would compare ourselves, and it didn't end there. I would watch how my dad treated other women and try to act like them because I wanted to receive all his attention.

Research from Marie Hartwell-Walker, EdD, from the *Psych Central* website states, "Regardless of whether he wants the responsibility, a father's relationship to the world and to women sets down a template that will be played out for another generation." My dad had no idea I was listening and watching his every move. What I experienced as a young girl is why I have struggled to connect with women. As a grown woman, I learned how to change my attitude to form better friendships because women are known to be distributors of love, compassion, and kindness.

MY PARENTS' FRIENDSHIPS

Do you remember watching your parents when their friends came over to visit? How did your parents interact with them?

I remember my parents laughing, dancing, arguing, and preparing meals together before their friends arrived at our home. Occasionally, my parents would wake us girls up to come to the living room to sing and dance for them. I hated being woken up to *perform* for people we didn't even know sometimes. It wasn't like we were getting paid to perform, even though we were very good at dancing—singing not so much.

It was always hard to go back to sleep, so we peeked out the crack of our bedroom door to watch all the action in our house. I noticed that there always seemed to be some drama going on in the background. As you can imagine, women didn't always get along back then, either. To this day, women are still jealous of each other. I would catch some of my mother's girlfriends being too friendly with my dad. My mom didn't like it much, and when she did notice, my parents would argue all night after everyone went home.

Sometimes things got to a point where my mother would try to beat up her girlfriend for disrespecting her home. Seeing women go at it with each other because of a man could confuse a young child. I couldn't understand what was happening because my mom and her best friend did everything together, and suddenly, they weren't even speaking. I learned that friendships were good until they were not.

That is why I always try to set boundaries early in a friendship because it does not take long for your best friend to turn into your worst enemy.

CONFLICT RESOLUTION

Friendships, just like any other relationship, will sometimes experience conflicts. How the conflict is resolved determines whether the friendship will fail or succeed. To ensure the friendship survives, here are some best mechanisms to resolve the conflicts:

- **Share Secrets:** To maintain friendships, honesty, trust, and concern for each other must be nurtured. This enables friends to share their secrets and other sensitive life experiences freely.

- **Boost Self-Confidence:** Boosting each other's self-confidence is very important in friendship. When supporting each other, helping to decrease one's self-doubts and insecurities shouldn't be a question.

- **Better Others:** Friendships provide a platform for people to feel relaxed and be willing to push one another to be their best. Great friends provide positive influence by dedicating their time to helping each other and are always ready to help one another realize their ambitions.

SAP TIME

What childhood memories do you recall?

Part 1 – Reason
(Friendship Develops)

"A person is in your life for a reason. It is usually to assist you through good and bad times. This person will offer their time, wisdom, and support. Be ready to receive it." – Tina Luckett

THE SEED

FRIENDSHIP CYCLE #1
The Seed

"A seed knows how to wait. Most seeds wait for at least a year before starting to grow." – Hope Jahren, Lab Girl

Have you ever wondered why it is hard to meet new people? You would think, as adults, we would have learned how to meet new people by now.

Here is a story my friend Leah shared with me:

Leah was rushing to her daughter's school, but she decided to stop and pick up dinner because she knew her daughter's dance rehearsal would run over. KFC was just one block down the road, and it wouldn't take too long for her to get there. Leah approached the counter to order her takeout. She noticed the only other customer in KFC frantically pulling stuff out of her purse and placing it on the counter. While waiting patiently, Leah overheard the conversation between the customer and the restaurant clerk.

"I'm sorry, I cannot believe I left my wallet at home," said the customer.

"I'm sure it's in your purse; try looking again," replied the restaurant clerk.

While Leah waited patiently, secretly hoping the customer would find her wallet soon, she couldn't help but peek over the customer's shoulder. She noticed that the customer's bill was twenty-four dollars and thirty-six cents. Leah looked at the time on her phone and realized she only had fifteen minutes to get her daughter to her dance rehearsal. Two minutes had passed, and the customer was still looking through each pocket of her purse. By this time, Leah's patience was running thin. On any other day, Leah wouldn't have minded waiting, but she couldn't that day.

Leah decided to rush the process along, so she asked the clerk if she could pay the tab. The customer turned around and stated, "No, you don't need to do that. I'll run home and grab my wallet. I don't have any ID on me, anyway. I'm just grabbing dinner and heading to my daughter's dance rehearsal."

"Me too," Leah replied. "It's no big deal."

"Are you sure? I promise to pay you back," said the customer.

"I will hold you to that. Now, let me order so we both won't be late to the rehearsal," Leah said. They both laughed.

Leah paid both bills, and they both made it to their daughters' dance rehearsals on time. Leah talked to the customer for the whole two hours while their daughters rehearsed. The ladies realized they had a lot in common, and their lives mirrored each other. They both had one child, and they both had been married before. The only difference was that the customer, Angel, was in the middle of a nasty divorce, while Leah had gotten divorced one year prior. Their husbands had left them for younger women.

Leah and Angel exchanged phone numbers, and they began to form a friendship. They talked a lot on the phone after that day. Most of the time, they had a lot to talk about because their daughters attended the same elementary school, and Leah could relate to what Angel was going through with her divorce proceedings. Leah was a shoulder for Angel to cry on during the rough days, and Angel was there for Leah when she decided to go back to college.

They met fifteen years ago and are still good friends today. You can never tell how far one act of kindness can go. Leah's understanding brought the two together for life. And not only did it bring *them* together, but their daughters are now roommates in college. Their encounter could've had an entirely different outcome if Leah had reacted differently. Imagine if she were angry and started talking rudely to Angel and the restaurant clerk. This could've upset Angel, and the friendship would not have happened. Always remain calm, be respectable, and help when needed because you never know how a friend may enter your life.

THE SEED

The Seed Friendship Cycle friend is the most important cycle. The PLANTING is where it all begins. It stems from the first sighting, the first notion to approach, and the first words between two strangers.

While people are brought together for many reasons, the goal is to meet new people who will support you. There are two types of seeds to look for while you are connecting and meeting new people: the good seed and the bad seed.

A good seed will help you grow as a person, while a bad seed will try to derail your growth process. Find the good seeds, and you will end up with a "forest of friends," not a "bush of twigs," because having solid friends around you is essential to continue on the right path to success.

THE BAD SEED

It is a given that you will be excited about connecting with new friends, and this could impair your judgment, so it's important to be more careful at this stage. Weeding out the bad seeds in your group will be necessary. When you plant seeds, you must water and pick out the weeds at some point. The same goes for your friendships; you must check on them. I have listed three steps below to help you become a better judge when picking friends.

Step #1 – Trust Your Gut

A woman's intuition is strong. The ability to sense or perceive is one of a woman's most substantial gifts. Pay attention to what God shows and whispers about people who shouldn't be in your life. Listen! You are not going crazy; that voice in your head is never wrong. My dad once told me, "When people show you who they are, believe them."

Step #2 – Recognize When Someone Doesn't Want You to Succeed

Some people will tell you they wish you success while secretly waiting for you to fail. Be cautious of what they tell you. People may say one thing, then do something totally differently. Believe their actions and what your intuition tells you.

Step #3 – Know the Warning Signs

1. A person who is *jealous* or *envious* will be hostile toward you because they think you have something they don't.
2. A person who *preys* on your weaknesses will use them against you. Be careful; this person is dangerous.
3. A person who *pretends* to like you can only pretend for so long. Watch everyone closely.
4. A person who *tries to get close to you too soon* will try to rush the friendship. There is no need to rush any relationship. It will blossom on its own. Have patience.

5. A person who *lies* will continue to lie repeatedly to keep you off guard. Stay alert.
6. A person who *wants what you have* would do anything in their power to "be" you. Do not share too much information too soon.
7. A person who *uses friendship to manipulate and control you* might turn a simple disagreement into an argument in ways that favor themselves. Do not allow someone to push their problems onto you.

Weeding out a bad seed is essential at the beginning of the friendship. While misery loves company, you can save yourself a lot of headaches if you look out for the signs listed above. The sooner you weed them out, the better your experience will be. You will not waste valuable time on people who only want to harm or use you. You deserve better.

The Seed Friendship Cycle is about meeting and connecting with people through different channels, such as work, family events, other friends, and social media, just to name a few. Catching up and reconnecting through social media can be a positive thing because all forms of connecting with others are important.

MEETING NEW FRIENDS AND CONVERSATION STARTERS

Research from the Mayo Clinic Staff shows that when it comes to meeting people, you may have overlooked potential friends already in your social network. Think of people you interact with regularly and write down their names. You will be surprised by how many people you are in contact with daily. Here are a couple of suggestions:

- People at your church
- Old classmates that you lost contact with
- Friends of other friends
- Your neighbors
- People who work in your building
- People at the daycare
- And the list goes on and on

Here are some conversation starters:

1. **Take the Lead**

   The next time you meet a new person or are introduced to someone again, try to connect by challenging yourself to start a quick conversation. You can start small and try striking up a conversation with someone new one day per week. After you get more comfortable, try two times per week.

   As you do this more, you will find that people are happy to talk with you about anything, including things like the weather, traffic, or how slow the grocery line is moving. You can even ask, "Have you been waiting long?" or compliment someone about their hair, makeup, outfit, or shoes. All of these are great conversation starters. I push myself to speak to everyone I meet. I try to make the most out of all my first encounters because you never know if that person will become vital later.

2. **Listen to Your Instincts**

   When you meet someone new, listen to your instincts. They will let you know if you have encountered a good seed or not; your instincts will not steer you wrong.

3. **Find a Common Ground**
   You will begin to recognize some of your different interests as you get to know each other. A seed does not compete with other seeds; it does not measure its growth by the growth of other seeds, even if exposed to the same resources simultaneously. The seed works within its own possibilities independent of whether it grows into a small or a big tree. It is the same with friendships. Your qualities or personal capabilities are not yardsticks for comparison but the unique dynamism present in each of us.

COMMUNICATION

In the Seed Friendship Cycle, committing to mastering the art of impeccable communication is a must. Tiffany Oakes from eLearning Best Practices states, "Communication is a topic that can be hard to master." She has listed 6 Tips for Communicating with Others:

1. **Really Listen.** Most of us do more talking than listening. Take the time to listen to what people say with their words, tone, and body language.
2. **Come Alongside the Other Person.** People don't need friends who beat them up; they need friends who help them out.
3. **Don't Give Unwanted Advice.** Do you have one of those friends who love to give you advice even when you don't ask for it? Most unwanted advice is just that—unwanted.
4. **Check Your Tone and Body Language.** Body language is more telling than the actual words you say. Therefore, watch your tone and body language when you are speaking.

5. **Be Real.** The best way to communicate is by being open and honest. If you are frustrated, say, "I'm frustrated." Labeling your feelings and working through them can help you when communicating with others.
6. **It's Not About You.** I hate to say it, but communicating isn't all about you. Communication is a two-way street; we must remember that the other person's thoughts and feelings are as important as our own.

Everything that Oakes talked about is the truth. I couldn't have said this better. People don't listen and think it's all about them. We need people to remember what's important to them.

For instance, you might have helped in your mom's garden and been excited to see the seeds turn into buds. Try to have that same excitement with your friendships because there is something about joy that encourages growth and creates an atmosphere where you can thrive.

Friendship is like a plant you want to grow—keeping it alive will be challenging because your seed will need plenty of water and sunlight, but with time comes greatness. Only sow your seed with people worthy of your friendship, and in time, you'll realize who deserves your energy.

SELF-REFLECTION

While attending a women's conference, my cousin introduced me to some of the ladies attending. I first noticed a nicely dressed lady who commanded attention when she entered the room. Everyone could see she was confident in herself.

I couldn't believe what I did next. Instead of appreciating my fellow woman, I turned my nose up at her. I'm not sure why I did, but I did. Was it right? No! I knew it wasn't right, but I didn't care. I needed to switch the attention to me, so I decided to talk *about* her outfit to other ladies around me.

How would she have felt if she knew what I was saying behind her back? That act was mischievous. It made no sense for me to feel the way I did. Why was I not happy to meet her? I wanted to discredit her from the moment I saw her. I don't understand why I was being so petty. I made a mistake and judged this woman before getting to know her, and I don't want you to make the same mistakes I have.

Sadly, we often have unpleasant feelings toward those we envision as competition to us—a sense of threat, as though they want to take our spot, the spot we never had. Someone once said, "Most of the things we feel jealous of or about are things we never desired in the first place." Too often, we focus on negative things. What I should've done was paid this woman a compliment. This is what a confident and strong woman would've done.

I learned from my research that I felt jealous of her at that moment because I wanted my ego satisfied. Will I behave in that manner again? Probably not. Now that I know better, I will do better. My friendships count on it.

I have also learned that the key to any new friendship is making the other person feel safe and allowing them to be themselves without being judged. According to Peter Wohlleben, author of *The Hidden Life of Trees*, "If you 'help' individual trees by getting rid of their supported competition, the remaining trees are bereft." He goes on to say, "Every tree now muddles along on its own… As a result, they are fit and grow better, but they aren't particularly long-lived. This is because a tree can be only as strong as the forest that surrounds it." If you want your friendship to work, surround yourself with great people and treat them like you would like to be treated, which is the ultimate rule of friendship.

The Seed Friendship Cycle is about meeting, connecting, building, and growing great friendships. No condemnation or competition allowed. Friends look to each other for validation and acceptance. Now *you* can be that friend who gives support. If you don't rush the friendship process, you will have a "forest of friends" you will be proud of.

SAP TIME

Have you met someone new lately?
What was the start of the conversation like?

_____

_____

_____

_____

_____

_____

_____

_____

_____

_____

_____

FINDING NEW FRIENDS
THE SEED FRIENDSHIP CYCLE

1. Before you can be a friend to others, you must first be a friend to yourself. Know that you cannot make others happy until you are happy.
2. Instead of looking for the right friend, look for *a friend*. Don't put that much pressure on yourself because no one will act or speak precisely as you envision.
3. Look for people who don't necessarily have the same interests as you. There can be common ground, but there should also be points of difference. You want someone who can teach you new things and increase your awareness. Having a diverse group of friends will keep you grounded.
4. Never put any barriers up before looking for a true friend. She's out there, and you will find her. Don't build up walls for new people to scale. Allow them to get to know you without having to break a leg to do so.
5. Be vulnerable. Let your friend see when you are hurting. Often, we are silent about what is bothering us, expecting the other person to miraculously unravel the mystery of our hurt. Don't be silent about things that matter because talking and sharing can strengthen your friendship.
6. Your seed will not grow unless you nurture it, so pour water and add fertilizer to your seeds daily. Time is an investment, so invest in your friends wisely.
7. Know that you're not alone in this conquest. Many people are looking for a friend just like you are.

FRIENDSHIP CYCLE #2
The Bark

"A friend doubles your joys and divides your sorrows." – Dr. John T. Chirban, a psychology professor at Harvard Medical School

Friendships are some of the most important connections we voluntarily make in our entire life. When people become friends, they always desire to see the friendship succeed. Proper care and attention are needed to grow the friendship and make it succeed. Healthy and strong friendships require trust, compassion, respect, and honesty.

Trust is one of the most critical elements and the foundation for lasting friendships. It may be easy to define, but we know it's the glue that holds the friendship together and keeps it going. Trust allows friends to feel safe when sharing life secrets. It requires one to keep their promise never to tell anyone.

Trust and confidence in a friend mean one can count on another to honor what they share with confidentiality and respect. We need loyalty, sincerity, honesty, and respect to develop a high level of trust in a friendship. It's very important in a friendship as it keeps friends together with a shared purpose and willingness to depend on each other. With trust, friends willingly contribute what is needed and share their dedication and honest thoughts.

When two people connect as friends, learning as much about each other as possible is imperative. This will create a better relationship.

When I met my best friend Annie at work in Colorado, I knew instantly that she was a person I wanted to get to know on a deeper level. She was kind, considerate, and respectful. I saw something in Annie that reminded me of myself, and because we took our time building our friendship, it paid off.

We talked a lot on the phone. We discovered that we had more in common than most. We love to cook, skate, and spend time with family and friends. But nothing can beat the trust and loyalty we have for each other. When I left my job and started working at a place near my home, Annie joined me. Some people have said we were inseparable, which we were until I moved to New Mexico and then to Michigan in 1999. Still, to this day, we talk, text, and email each other every week. I value Annie's friendship very much because she has made me a better person—having our husbands become great friends was a bonus for us.

I was fortunate to have met two of my other best friends at work. Shortly after moving to Michigan, I met Edie and Lisa. We worked at the same food company together. Edie and Lisa worked there at different times, so they don't know each other well, but their personalities are similar, and that's what I love about them both. I can call either one of these ladies and know they will be there for me no matter what. This is the type of friend I look for—the friend that knows me better than I know myself. These three ladies are my "ride or die" friends. They will be taking all my secrets to their grave.

THE BARK

The Bark Friendship Cycle friend is the most interesting. The DISCOVERY is where you will uncover the good and bad things about your new friend. Here you can peel back each layer of your friend's character: seeing her vulnerability and understanding where she has been and where she is going.

In this cycle, you will continue to learn about each other, just like in the Seed cycle. Sometimes you are going to get along, and sometimes you are not. Your relationship will have its share of ups and downs until you get to know each other's likes and dislikes. You must take the time to get to know your friend, so you will have each other to lean on and conquer the world together. Be open-minded and impartial, and your friend will appreciate your kindness and strength when she's weak. So, remember, your friendship will be tested the most here because, to have a friend, *you must be a friend first*!

I like this cycle because you have the chance to share some special moments and get to know a person on a deeper level. The deeper you go, the better the relationship will work. Being vulnerable is a strength, not a weakness.

As you peel back those layers with your friend, prepare yourself, because you might not like what you see. However, regardless of what you uncover, you should be able to get through it together. If not, you must decide if you should continue this friendship. Remember, you're entirely in control and must determine what kind of friend you want to be around.

So, hang in there! Everyone comes into a relationship with baggage, so be prepared to help each other overcome obstacles. Who knows, she might be the one you have been waiting for. Don't be the one who is exhausted in a relationship; instead, focus on the goal of becoming a valuable friend. Here you will be getting to the root of many problems.

This is where you can enlist your friends to help you because you should not be on a one-way street alone. Take the two-way highway instead and continue your path to greatness together. Trust in her, and she will believe in you. This will not be the time to give up; instead, double down on the relationship. This book will prepare you for those moments.

TRUST

Trust is so important in a friendship. The common reasons people find it hard to trust each other include having a low propensity to trust, unrealistic expectations, past hurts that may be holding one back, a belief that everyone only protects themselves, social media, publicity of cheating, gossip, and being uncomfortable with vulnerability among others.

To combat these challenges, people should strive to build lasting friendships by considering the qualities listed below:

- **Transparency:** Share information, i.e., thoughts and feelings. Lack of transparency causes people to assume the worst.
- **Reliability and dependability:** Nurture trust, remain true to their word, and fulfill their commitments.
- **Openness and vulnerability:** Explore your fears and talk about them.

BEST FRIENDS FOREVER

You know you are not alone if you have a best friend. You understand that no matter what, you will have someone to walk you through any fire. Your friend will guide you in the right direction, take the heat off others, and show you unconditional love. You cannot put a price on friendship with a sense of purpose and belonging. The gratitude of the other person is genuine.

Identify who your best friend truly is:

Here are seven questions to keep in mind:

THE 7 FRIENDSHIP CYCLES

1. **Is your friend judgmental?**
   When things don't go as planned, how does she react? Does she always look for a chance to bring you down? An ideal friend will not quickly put you in a judgmental box. Your best friend is someone you can call upon when you seem to be losing it. Such a friend will not exploit the situation or think less of you.

2. **Is your friend completely honest with you?**
   Does your friend show integrity, truthfulness, and straightforwardness? Or does she lie, steal, or cheat her way through the friendship instead? Either way, a true friend will always look forward to your success and improved progress. She wouldn't hesitate to tell you the truth or speak her mind, even if it meant telling you you were wrong. Something is wrong if your friend would rather text you superficially than have a serious conversation. Ideal friends look forward to talking things out.

3. **How much respect does your friend have for you?**
   A true friend has seen you at your worst and yet respects you for it. She may not nod every time you raise an opinion. However, she will always respect you for that opinion. Respect is vital in a relationship, so always treat your friends with respect no matter what. When you respect each other, others will appreciate the both of you. A friendship that brings you insult is no friendship at all.

4. **Does your friend forgive you when you err?**
   It is hard to forge ahead in any friendship when one party is forever clinging to the past. In other words, being a best friend is more than forgiveness; it is about being empathic

when it matters and putting yourself in your friend's shoes. Likewise, your best friend comprehends that you are imperfect and committed to your self-improvement, and a good friend will recognize your truthfulness.

5. **Does your friend support you?**
   Is she available when you call, or does she pretend to be busy? Real friends will offer their time and attention whenever the need arises. They don't just do it; they do it excitedly.

6. **How good is your friend at acknowledgment?**
   We all need people to share the great moments of our lives when something significant happens. Does your friend call to share their joy when those beautiful moments show up? Are you invited when those "shining occasions" happen to her? An ideal friend will look forward to sharing such great moments with you. If she ponders or brings up negative things in these great moments, then you probably were not good friends in the first place.

7. **How reliable is your friend?**
   There are certain people in life we can turn to when all is lost. They have repeatedly been there through good and bad times. They were not just there; they gave you their back to ride on. While other people go around telling all who care to listen how much they have helped you, such a friend never seeks to be known as your "bail-out" person.

SAP TIME

How much do you know about your best friend?

DIG DEEPER
THE BARK FRIENDSHIP CYCLE

1. Take the time to get to know people. They will help you grow.
2. Do you feel like you can say whatever you want around your friend?
3. Can you trust your friend? If not, find out why.
4. Can you be yourself around others?
5. Know that you are always in control. It's all right to let your guard down; it will only help you to build trust.
6. If you're still struggling at this point, you probably don't have a best friend yet. Keep searching; time is on your side.
7. Share your special moments; there is enough room for both of you.

Part 2 – Season
(Friendship Choices)

"A person appears in your life for a season; they could make you smile or shed a tear. Their time with you will be limited, so enjoy the time you have together."
– Tina Luckett

FRIENDSHIP CYCLE #3
The Branch

Spanish philosopher Baltasar Gracian once said, "Strive to have friends, for life without friends is like life on a desert island... To find one real friend in a lifetime is good fortune; to keep him is a blessing."

If we believe what Gracian said, then some of us will be blessed enough to find one great friend, while the rest of us will be stuck on a desert island for a long while.

Sometimes life takes us in different directions only to bring us back to where we started. Take my high school friend, Patty, for instance. Patty and I signed up for the military as "military buddies." As military buddies, we thought we would be kept together throughout our military careers, just like our recruiter promised. Patty entered the service one year before me because I failed my military exam. I failed, and I'm still shaking my head about that. I promised Patty I would catch up with her after completing my basic training, but that never happened.

After completing my training, I was sent to Germany, and Patty went to Korea. After our overseas tours, I was sent to Louisiana, and she got stationed in Georgia. We were never in the same place at the same time, even after we both decided to get out of the military years later. Even after life took us in different directions, we remained close friends after all these years, though I now live in Michigan, and she still lives in Georgia.

Branching out in different directions is not necessarily a bad thing. It works for Patty and me and could work for you too.

THE BRANCH

The Branch Friendship Cycle friend is where most major decisions will be made. The DIRECTION is where the friendship will come to a crossroad. You will need to decide which road to take.

The Branch Friendship Cycle friend has a direct personality, and handling their blunt and straightforward approach will take a lot. There will be confusion from time to time, and your emotions will play a big part here. When you are in this cycle, the friendship could go either way. If she likes you, she will let you know. If not, you will know that too. How much you get out of the friendship will depend on your will to survive it.

However, it will be all right if you decide not to continue the friendship. You probably will not hurt anyone because the friendship is still fairly new. Ending it now will likely benefit both of you because you haven't put much effort into continuing it.

Remember, I mentioned earlier that you will need to make some major decisions in this cycle. This cycle is also important because it can make or break the friendship. The relationship might be up and down at times, but if you're not a strong-willed person, the branch will stretch out over you. This friend will run the friendship, and that's not what you want. Friendships should go in two directions, and you both should be in the driver's seat in order to sustain longevity.

Even though branches can grow in many directions, I believe they have a mutual understanding with other branches. There is no pushing for space, and they protect each other by staying in their own space. The branches allow sufficient room between each other for the wind and air to have enough space to pass through. Unfortunately, people don't always do the same.

Wohlleben said it best: "Even strong trees get sick, and this is the time when they depend on their weaker neighbors." So, dig down and hold on tight. There are going to be bumpy roads ahead, but it is nothing you cannot handle. So, don't take it personally if you notice a friend snaps at you when you call. Whatever she is going through likely has nothing to do with you if you have been a great friend. You will need to be there for her during these times, though. Everyone has a bad day from time to time, and if you can endure the rough roads, you will be headed toward a beautiful place.

While in that beautiful place, you will need to tell the truth, no matter the consequences. Some people will be able to handle this; others won't. For the friendship to stay in this cycle, this person must be consistent and not hesitate to tell her friend what others are afraid to say. These tough conversations will only grow the relationship and allow anyone involved to develop a thick skin.

It would help to treat a friend in the Branch cycle like a pair of shoes. Occasionally, you grab that pair of cute shoes and walk into a room, feeling confident, excited, and demanding the attention of everyone at the party. Now, no matter what happens that night, you know your feet will be hurting by the end of it. So, as you put that pair of shoes back in the closet, think about how painful it was to walk around in those shoes all night. With each step, the pain worsens, but that doesn't stop you from wearing them. Now, compare that pain with your friends; no matter what happens in the friendship, you keep returning for more abuse. Sometimes in your relationships, you will need to put your friends back in their place. It doesn't take much for a friend to get comfortable with the relationship and believe you will allow her to treat you poorly. So, to keep things civil, state your clear expectations for the friendship to continue. Do not be afraid of losing her. If your friendship is meant to be, it will become stronger than before.

However, if the relationship is not strong and she blames you for messing up this "fake" relationship, life will continue with or without your former best friend. Do you know the line from R&B singer Toni Braxton's song that says, "Love Shoulda Brought You Home"? This friendship should have brought you closer, but it didn't. There are times when you have that friend that gets on your nerves. You know the one I am referring to. I'm sure you have one too. The friend that complains about everything only thinks about herself and puts others last. We all have one in our lives. If that person is draining the energy out of you, dump her.

THE SEASONAL FRIEND

Some friendships are not meant to be forever; these are our "seasonal friends." God puts people in our lives to help us get through certain things. These friendships will end when it is time to move on. This does not mean you didn't like that person; it means their services are no longer needed, and that is also all right. This is when you should use your time wisely. You may not always know immediately if this person is a seasonal friend or one who will stay the course and become a lifelong friend, but be aware of your time within all friendships. Your time is valuable, and you do not want to waste it on the wrong person.

I once had a friend who only thought about herself. She would call me every day and only talk about her life. It was not that I did not want to hear about her problems, but it caused an issue when I would try to interject my own stories. She would rudely talk over me and did not care what I had to say. If your friend is only interested in topics she brings up, you might want to rethink this entanglement. At some point, you need to consider your own happiness.

I am at a stage right now where I prioritize my happiness over others who do not give a "ham" about me. It is okay to put yourself first as long as you are not putting others down. Ideally, you will achieve a balance of friendships and not waste time investing in fruitless endeavors. Do not stick with toxic people who are time wasters; learn to balance your view on life and things in general.

The Branch cycle is very flaky, so to survive, either you will enjoy the ride or not. The choice is up to you. Life will go on, and you deserve to be surrounded by people who will appreciate your presence.

There are people out there who want something from you to be your friend. The key in these situations is to excuse yourself when someone treats you like the gum on the bottom of their shoes. You deserve better; demand it.

Here are Four Steps to Analyzing and Re-Evaluating Your Relationship:

1. **The Principle of Empathy.** Always seek to look at things from your friend's perspective. They can have great ideas too.
2. **Look for Your Why.** Serve and bolster your friend. Do not be a liability. How are you able to improve her situation? How might you help? What could you add to her life to improve it? This question will give you your "why."
3. **Process Your Thoughts Before Sharing Them.** Think before you say something—especially if you are irate. A lot

of times, pausing for a moment or two to examine what you want to say makes all the difference. Pick your words mindfully.
4. **Take Responsibility for Your Friendship.** Meet regularly and hang out. If there is an issue, recognize your part and decide how to correct it. It will lag when neither individual is watching out for the relationship.

LISTENING

Listening is an important skill to master. Being a great listener is essential for many reasons. For one, it shows a genuine interest when you care enough to listen. Two, I once heard someone say people do not listen to understand or retain but to get information. Having exceptional listening skills will attract people to you because everyone wants to be heard. Effective listening gives you an advantage when creating and maintaining friendships and helps your friends feel important. When you have some good news, who do you call first? You call your best friend, right?

The average person gets sick of people pretending to listen. What would you call a person who always enjoys talking and never listening? A RUDE INDIVIDUAL!

How well does your best friend enjoy listening to you? A true friendship entails both people listening to each other. The Branch can be a great listener as well. A true friend is always there to provide an immense amount of comfort and support.

There is a need for mutual communication and response in any healthy relationship. It would help if you had someone who would listen to you attentively and not judge you. Moreover, the quality of a person's advice or response depends on the quality of listening. It is unhealthy to keep investing in a friendship where the other party never listens. Being a great listener makes a friendship tighter.

There is nothing like having someone sit and listen while you pour your heart out. It shows compassion and that they care. Sometimes your friend may not even have anything to say that can solve the issue outright, but a friend with good listening skills melts the heaviness in your heart.

However, be aware of your tone when speaking because your tone dictates the mood of the conversation. Nothing is worse than someone taking your tone out of context. When one is talking without being tuned in to what the other person is saying, it is evident that there is no relationship—and the same goes should you be the one doing the talking. Be mindful; listening goes a long way.

SAP TIME

*There will come a time when you need to make tough decisions.
What tough decisions have you made this month?
Did it hurt or help your friendships?*

FOLLOW THE SIGNS
THE BRANCH FRIENDSHIP CYCLE

1. What are you looking for in a friendship?
2. Don't be afraid to make that tough decision when you get to that crossroads.
3. Do you do more talking or listening in this friendship?
4. Be willing to help your friend.
5. Do you get mad if she does not pick up the phone when you call?
6. Do not be the weakest link; stand out.
7. Before you end any friendship, ensure you have exhausted all avenues and given it your best effort.

FRIENDSHIP CYCLE #4
The Vine

"If friends disappoint you over and over, that's in large part your own fault. Once someone has shown a tendency to be self-centered, you need to recognize that and take care of yourself; people aren't going to change simply because you want them to." – Oprah Winfrey

There's no secret; your friends will disappoint you over and over again. The question is, what are you going to do about it?

I had a friend who kept blaming me for her shortcomings. Even though I don't want to see any of my friends down, sad, or in this case, delusional, I want the best for them. However, at some point, if you keep doing the same thing, you will continue to receive the same result. I know we've all heard that saying before, and it's still true today. As much as I wanted to help this friend, it was never enough. I realized that she wasn't ready to make any changes.

I continued to be there for her, but her problems and drama started becoming mine after a while. So, I took Ms. Winfrey's advice to "take care of yourself." It was a hard decision, but I had to let our friendship go because it started affecting my health and well-being.

Do I miss her? Of course, I do, but I love myself more, and it's all right to feel that way. I'm not being selfish; I'm being smart.

My new model is to stop allowing others to drag you into their drama! Stay in your own lane, and don't be other people's doormats. Put out your own doormat; it will look better at your home anyway.

THE VINE

The Vine Friendship Cycle friend is the most confusing and dangerous. The BREAKDOWN is where many friendships will gain confidence to get rid of toxic people who are choking the life out of them.

The Vine Friendship Cycle friend can be slippery as a snake. She may be a backstabbing bitch at times, so you will need to watch your back before you get bit. The Vine has two functions in this stage: it can be a blessing by carrying the nutrients to produce fruit or a nuisance to hang you out to dry.

Will your friend be your nutrient or a nuisance? You should ask yourself: does my friend add joy to my life or divide my sorrows? It is an easy question, but it might be harder to answer. However, these questions must be asked for the friendship to move forward. No one said friendships were easy. They require time and putting others before yourself; some people may have a problem with that.

Being in this cycle can be bad for your health. You don't want to stay in this cycle for too long. Vines can be very needy. Your friend will call and complain about her life and never ask about yours throughout the conversation. Letting her know you no longer want to be her sounding board is okay. At some point, you will need to take control of the friendship. It hurts to keep giving without receiving anything in return. If there is ever a time to cut off a friendship, this will be the cycle where that should occur. Unlike the Branch Friendship Cycle, where the friendship could survive if both parties work toward fixing it, it is not so easy with the Vine friend. You want to believe that a person would not dig very deep to hurt you, but they will.

CUTTING OFF FRIENDSHIPS

According to content writer Sarah Marie Williamson at the University of South Carolina-Aiken, "When the roles of giver and taker become obviously distinct, it is time to rethink the benefits of keeping the latter as a friend. In female friendships, especially, communication is key. However, if you have a friend who only shows interest in the issues they introduce, it is instinctive to doubt his or her interest in you."

People will occupy relationships with their drama. Be careful because a person in this Vine cycle will always have some mess going on. There will always be drama and never a time of silence. Before you know it, you will be tangled in something that has nothing to do with you. Their drama will take over your life. It will feel like an endless cycle that will go around and around until you have enough guts to stop it.

In some cases, this will last for years. React quickly, or you will waste half your life trying to fix an unfixable relationship. Misery loves company; however, you do not need to participate. According to Oprah Winfrey, Kelly Diels stated, "You can't be friends with someone who wants your life." It is hard to be a Vine's friend. You will be called upon to put yourself last. This might work for some, but it may not work for most. Eventually, you must put down your foot and re-evaluate your relationship.

I remember my ex-friend (let's call her Sunday). She pretended to be my friend, so I would let her into my small circle. I trusted her, and I liked her a lot. I noticed that my photos of my husband and I would be facedown occasionally. It bothered me, and I couldn't figure out who hated me enough to keep turning my wedding picture facedown. I would've never thought it was Sunday in a lifetime. I trusted her with my life. One day, she was over with a couple more of my friends. I had to run upstairs to grab something, and when I was returning, I decided to peek over my balcony. What I saw shook me to my core. Sunday stood near the photos; she kissed one, then forcefully knocked it over.

When I returned to the group, I told the ladies how my photo kept being facedown, and I didn't know why. Of course, Sunday was the first to add her advice. She suggested I remove all the photos because people did not believe we were a happy couple. What the hell!!! After that night, I decided that we would no longer be friends. The trust was gone. I'm still unsure why she kissed the photo; maybe she kissed my husband's side. It was weird.

Breaking up with a friend is the worst, I know. Most of us fear breaking off a relationship in person because blocking or unfriending someone on social media is much easier. Learning how to move on will be hard, but it is not about how many friends you have but how many bring value to your life.

DECLUTTERING

Having a friend should make you happy, not sad. It is hard to maintain friendships with people who take you for granted. To get along in this cycle, respect other people's opinions and don't put them down. It would be best if you always watched how you talk to someone and remember people have different backgrounds and cultures, so treat everyone fairly.

Suzanne Degges-White, Ph.D., a licensed counselor at Northern Illinois University, stated, "Research shows that friendships that bring us down or create conflict are worse for our well-being than having fewer friendships in total. Choose to cleanse your life of toxic friends who support poor behaviors and let go of the people who encourage you to stay down with them."

That is the best advice I could give someone struggling with letting go. Letting go will free you to open your heart and soul to find a pool of friends with better qualities.

The key is to pay attention to what season you are in. God put people in your life to advance you to the next level, not drag you down with their negativity. Your time is valuable, and you must use it wisely.

MOVING ON

It is time to clean out all the closets and get rid of the clutter. This is what you must do when it comes to your friendships. It is entirely all right to realign and evaluate your friendships. If you want to have a drama-free life, it is time to say "Bye, Felicia" to some folks. It's nothing personal; it's just part of life.

SAP TIME

Is your best friend adding nutrients or becoming a nuisance in your life?

_____

_____

_____

_____

_____

_____

ENDING FRIENDSHIPS
THE VINE FRIENDSHIP CYCLE

1. Make a list of the things you like and don't like about your friend. If the "do nots" outweigh the "dos," it is time to end the friendship.
2. It is all right to cut the vines and grow new ones.
3. If you are always angry and upset at this person, it is time to end the friendship.
4. Decide if this relationship is hurting you or helping you advance as a person. If it hurts you, you must dissolve the relationship ASAP. You will feel lighter, relieved, and filled with an abundance of joy to know that you have made the right decision.
5. If she is sucking up all your time and you are fed up, it is time to end the friendship.
6. You must decide whether your friendship is a liability or an asset. If it's a liability, don't waste your time. If it's an asset, list the value it adds and keep it moving. It's that simple.
7. Don't continue the same routine because you will get the same results. Cut people off, and don't look back.

Part 3 – Lifetime
(Friendship Goals)

"A person will be here for a lifetime. This person will weather the storm with you, teach you lessons, and build lasting friendships. Love this person with all your heart; they have your back." – Tina Luckett

THE LEAF

FRIENDSHIP CYCLE #5
The Leaf

"A friend like 'a sheltering tree'? A friend who takes second place without jealousy and cheers loudly and sincerely as you stand above him on the podium. A friend who affirms and encourages, who stands by you loyally even when passed over."
– Scott Whitaker from Impact for Living

What is a sheltering tree? Samuel Taylor Coleridge wrote a poem titled "Youth and Age," where he mentioned, "Friendship is a sheltering tree." It took me some time to research what that meant, but Canadian Certified Counsellor Ruth Bergen Braun might have said it best: "You may live in a forest of sheltering friends. Or, have just one lone tree—a good friend who shelters you from the storm."

My best friends Lois, LaTisha, Sandy, Rose, and I all could be "sheltering trees." Any of them would be happy to come in second place to me, and I feel the same about them. We would definitely shield each other. Even though I don't talk to them every day, you wouldn't know it because we pick right up where we left off when I do. Finding good friends is hard, but when you do, work hard to keep them.

THE LEAF

The Leaf Friendship Cycle friend is the most common. The SHIELD OF PROTECTION is where the friendship develops even if you haven't spoken to each other in months. As you navigate this cycle, you will continue moving the friendship forward.

A Leaf friend will drop everything to be that shelter for her friends. She will be the one who pushes them to go after their dreams and supports whatever they want to be. She is not jealous of others' success. I read online, "A best friend is like a four-leaf clover—hard to find, and you are lucky to have one." That is a Leaf friend: once you find her, you will have a friend who will protect your feelings, emotions, and secrets for a lifetime.

This is my favorite cycle because I know I will not be alone if I'm going through something. Even though most of my friends say that I'm their root, I know I'm also their Leaf because I have no problem blowing into their lives when the need arises and blowing out when the situation is under control. I prefer it this way because I have a lot of friends, and I cannot be around each of them all the time, so I'm the type of friend who will occasionally call, text, or send a card unless I'm needed in person, then I will be there.

There are going to be times when you drift apart. For instance, you may get married, enroll in school, or move to another state, but you are never too far to offer support or advice, no matter the change. Putting others first is the Leaf's main priority. When we think of others and their wellness, we find our way to a life of total peace and wholesomeness.

When you are in this Leaf Friendship Cycle, don't feel bad or guilty about not talking every day. When you get together with your friend, you will not struggle to find anything to talk about because it will feel like old times, and you will spend hours catching up. Just know that you will be there for each other when needed. That is what real friends do for each other.

While in this cycle, the friendship will continue to grow stronger. Here are three tips to help:

1. **Set Apart Ample Time for Your Friend.** Invest in your friendship. One way to show your commitment to your friendship is by setting apart quality time for your friend. No matter how busy you are, you will create time if you are committed to that friendship. Show your friend that *you value their friendship*.

2. **Tune In.** Develop a genuine interest in what the other person is communicating. Ask questions so she can know that you are listening. You never know how far this simple gesture can go in a friendship. Maintaining eye contact and nonverbal cues are vital methods for showing you are genuinely paying attention.

3. **Celebrate Your Friends for Who They Are.** Congratulate your friends on their accomplishments, promotions, and even struggles. Let them know you accept them for who they are, not who you wish them to be.

DISTANCE

Do you have that one friend that you don't talk to often, but when you do, you both pick up where you left off? I always think about my friend Annie, but I cannot call her as much as I would like with my busy schedule. I like that she doesn't give me a hard time when I call. I know she sees photos of me hanging out with my other friends on social media, but she never gets jealous or envious of me.

According to Williamson, "Even the best of friends might end up only seeing each other once a month or texting to keep the interaction alive. Distance and separation strengthen and help friendships mature, but only if everyone involved is seriously dedicated to making time for one another." Having a friend who understands why I don't invite her to all my events and still calls me her best friend makes me appreciate our friendship and allows us to continue building what we call our "friendship forest."

In the Leaf Friendship Cycle, long-distance relationships work well. Not having constant contact daily will not hinder the relationship because the key is to be supportive, which will keep the friendship bond intact. The Leaf is your *shield of protection* and *your ally in conquering all the things that are not good for you*. If a tear falls, she will be there with a Kleenex to wipe it away. That is the definition of true friendship.

You're on the right track if you can find three Leaves in a lifetime. I was fortunate enough to find mine. Becoming friends with my Leaves wasn't easy; connecting, building, and managing our relationships took a lot. However, I'm in a better place because of all the commitment we put in to make it work. These ladies are my rocks, and I love them all.

A TRUE FRIEND

George Washington once said, "True friendship is a plant of slow growth and must undergo and withstand the shocks of adversity before it is entitled to the appellation."

Friendship is an essential part of our lives. We cannot sustain ourselves as human beings independent of one another. Despite the vast responsibilities and commitments they place on us, friendships are essential and important. True friends are close partners and loyal regardless of how enticing the rewards of betrayal might be, and is not afraid of what they will lose or what is at stake for standing with you. They are dependable and are not "frenemies."

A true friend is like having a cell phone. It is always in eye range, always on and ready to go, and will help you find your way through any miscommunication if you ask Siri or Alexa. A cell phone provides an incredible array of functions, such as a two-way communication portal, like the one between two lifetime friends. As with any important things in your life, your most valuable friends are in your "favorites" folder, and you might have them on speed dial. When the wireless signal is strong, there will be no disconnections. Similarly, a true friend is the glue of the relationship; she will hold the connection together.

A true friend is someone you love being around each day. This person doesn't mind being in your shadow. This person will help you find your destiny in life. A true friend is someone that God has sent to watch over you. This person will let you be you! This person will provide encouragement, humor, and empathy. Such friendships are indeed reliable, and they are spiced with doses of responsibility that go both ways. A true friend will call to say hello and not expect anything in return.

A friend for life will share hopes, dreams, and discouragements with you. A true friend will tell you the truth and not beat around the bush, even when it hurts. Conversely, an untrue friend will let you fail.

True friends are faithful; they stay by you through it all. These steadfast friends are committed to the people in their lives.

SAP TIME

When did you last check on a friend you have not seen in a while?

MOVING THE FRIENDSHIP FORWARD
THE LEAF FRIENDSHIP CYCLE

1. Keep the lines of communication open.
2. Call your friend when problems arise; she will be there to help.
3. Don't keep any secrets from each other. Being truthful and honest will make for an unbreakable bond and Girl Power!
4. Stay true to yourself. Always show your true colors, and don't worry about what others think.
5. You may not talk with each other every day, and that is all right.
6. Respect others' time and listen attentively.
7. Trust your gut. If the friendship doesn't feel right, it might not be right.

FRIENDSHIP CYCLE #6
The Root

"My best friend is the one who brings out the best in me."
– Henry Ford

Friendship is the most valuable asset in a person's life, and it amazes me how few people make it through this cycle. Having someone in your corner who supports and is there for you is invaluable; it is truly a blessing. Finding a best friend you can call on forever takes a special kind of skill. Your best friends and close friends are your true soul mates.

Only ten of my friends have made it to this cycle. Cat, Debra, Ederique, Antoinette, Sharon, LaTeesh, Rosa, Bean, Patrice, and Lisha.

THE ROOT

The Root Friendship Cycle friend is the most authentic. The ROCK is someone you can put all your trust in. You will be able to tell her everything. She is mature, trustworthy, and reliable. You will call this person when you need help, support, and advice. She will have your back, and you will have hers.

The Root friend is someone who will drop everything to be your sounding board, your companion, and your bodyguard. You will sleep comfortably in this cycle, knowing someone loves you like their sister. It is safe to say that you are like an open book, and your friend is not afraid to *read* the pages.

Finding someone who is the Root will be hard. For someone to be your Root, you must have established the bond for years or even decades. This person doesn't just stroll into your life; they have been in it for a long time. This type of friendship has had time to cultivate from the inside out, starting at the core. Do not be surprised if you only have a few friends in your life whom you can call your "Root." Finding real friends is like finding a diamond in a pile of broken glass; it is possible, and you will find it.

Friends you can count on and trust go together like peanut butter and jelly. It makes a great sandwich and makes you smile after each bite. As you spend time creating the balances and checks for others to be good friends, are you investing in yourselves to ensure you have the same qualities?

This type of person would jump in front of a bullet for you. Would you do the same for them? I have many faithful, loyal, and true friends who would take a bullet for any of them. I did jump in front of a gun for one of my high school friends. I always get in trouble, even when I'm just minding my business.

Here is what happened. It was a typical day at school. All the kids were walking toward the bus stop when I heard a girl yell, "Stop, or I will shoot." I wasn't sure who the girl was talking to, so I kept walking, but I was praying she wasn't talking to me. I noticed all the other students running toward the bus, so I began running.

As I looked back to see how close the girl who was yelling was, I saw my friend Gina running toward the bus. Luckily for Gina, I asked the bus driver to wait for her. I felt relieved as Gina ran up the steps.

Frightened, I yelled at the driver to close the door. He wasn't fast enough because the girl with a shiny object in her hand also ran up the steps. The bus driver raised his arms in the air. The girl with the shiny object was a few feet away from me. Gina had managed to scoot past me and ended up to the left of me, looking frightened as hell.

At that moment, I thought, *Why did I run on the bus?* As I turned toward the girl, it only took a second to realize the shiny object was a nine-millimeter pistol, and it was pointed in my direction. I saw my life flash before me. If you have ever had a gun pointed at you, trust me, you would see your life flash before you too. So many things were running through my head; for instance, I forgot to tell my dad I loved him before leaving home that morning.

I knew someone had to take control of the situation. Why I decided to be brave this day, only God knows. I didn't know the girl personally but had seen her around the school. I think her name was Pam. She was quiet, always alone, and never bothered anyone. And yet, here I was, staring down the barrel of a gun; I felt sick. I could feel my bacon, egg, and cheese coming back up.

This was back in the eighties. There were no cell phones, so I couldn't call the police or my father. I was terrified. I asked Pam why she was holding a gun in my face, and she explained that Gina and her friends were bullying her.

"Gina who?" I said, my voice trembling. I was shocked. Not my friend Gina. No way! I was a good friend of Gina's, and I had never seen her bully anyone.

I tried to talk things out with Pam, but she wouldn't listen. I warned her that she could spend the rest of her life in prison if she didn't put the gun down. I could see in her eyes that she didn't want to use it, but this was something she was pushed to do. She probably thought it was her only way out.

While all this was happening, big bad Gina cried like a baby. She wasn't so tough now without her other friends around. Even though I was one of her friends, I had no idea she had been bullying people. I never saw her act this way, and I was unhappy. I was hoping this wasn't true.

Although it seemed like a lifetime, it was only about four minutes when Pam decided to put the gun away. She got off at the next stop. I saw something in her eyes and knew she didn't want to hurt anyone, including Gina. I didn't want Pam to be alone, so I got off too. But before exiting, I told Gina we would talk about this incident later.

I learned a lot about Pam that day, and I think she also learned a lot about me. I knew that we should sometimes put others' feelings before our own. In this case, Gina and her friends hadn't done that, and Pam was willing to take Gina's life to make her pain disappear.

The next day, I had a long talk with Gina. I told her I was not too fond of her behavior and that we would no longer be friends if it continued. After that day, Gina and her friends never bothered Pam again. Sadly, after graduating high school and joining the military, I lost contact with both ladies.

So, the moral of the story is you never know what a person is going through and what they can do if they are pushed to their limit. If you treat others like they want to be treated, then you will always be in the right.

SETTING STANDARDS

A standard is a set of values and perspectives that guide you on how you carry on with your life. One standard could be excellence, another could be integrity, and another could be optimism. These standards are the lens through which you examine everything in your life.

What are your values? What are your standards? To change the quality of your friendships, set higher standards. It is simple. These things have a way of touching every aspect of your life.

Put yourself in the shoes of others; in all sincerity, would you want to be your friend? No one wants a mediocre person for a friend. Every friend with big goals wants a friend headed in her direction. There is no vacuum in friendships; your friend will either inspire you to greatness or inspire you to mediocrity. Aspiring to low norms will undermine your potential. Nothing just happens. You were designed to thrive by your choice and your vision.

Your standards set the tone for your vision, and this vision drives every other thing. Napoleon Hill said it best: "Whatever the mind can conceive and believe, it can achieve." Individuals with low aspirations run on low motivational energy and take life as it is. However, a person with expectations as high as the sky is completely immersed in her ambitions. Her eyes are set on the prize. She is on fire. As a result, she gives her all to get the best in life—including gaining the best of friendships.

According to reports, people who set high standards for themselves usually feel great about themselves and others. Psychology reveals that such folks have high self-esteem. They understand that, in life, there is more than enough for everybody, and indeed everyone can win. These individuals usually draw others in with their big visions and tend to wave off pessimistic people and avoid them at all costs. Their exclusive insight keeps them far from pessimism. Individuals with high expectations are sensitive to friendships and connections. Individuals with big visions have much to lose should they tangle with the wrong person; hence, your input in personal development matters strongly.

What goals have you set for yourself? What keeps you moving every waking hour? What are those qualities that separate you from other people? What kind of person do you want to see in five, ten, fifteen, or even twenty years when you look into the mirror? This will affect everything else in your life, including your friendships.

Commit to constant personal development and see if you attract the right friends. Raise the bar for your goals and exceed the limits of your aspirations. We become what we behold. Commit to improving your capacity; you will attract folks going in your direction. The standards you set affect your well-being, soul, relationships, and success in life.

Begin putting principles in place by taking a critical look at things. The way to a fruitful life is to set a higher standard for something. Look at characterizing benchmarks that propel your development as an individual—they should be some things that you genuinely need. If you set an excessive number of principles, you risk being disappointed. Select just three and ensure they are the ones that are most imperative to you.

Having high standards for yourself will help you achieve a good relationship with others. Having high standards will affect and influence so many people around you. By having high standards, you will become the alpha in a group. You will set the pace of that friendship.

As you interact with your friend, you will develop respect for one another and others around you. However, the more influence or prestige a person has over their friendship, the higher their status will rise within this cycle. For example: if your friend is an attorney or doctor, she will make herself the "alpha" of the pack. Other people might try to follow in her steps. However, watch out for friends who do not like where they are in life and might feel excluded from the pack.

Molding a friendship is like having a leader's influence over others. It is like shaping something you care for and being around people you care about, guiding people in the right direction, having the power to produce actions, and positively influencing others' opinions. When you use your natural ability to get along with others, it is a win-win relationship. And as we know, life is about relationships. The better you can work with someone, the better you will understand that person.

SAP TIME

Having a lifetime friend is a blessing; do not ruin it with your self-doubt. Finding a friend at this stage is beyond anything you have dreamt it would be.

BEING THE ROCK
THE ROOT FRIENDSHIP CYCLE

1. Would you jump in front of a bullet to save someone's life?
2. Does your friend give good advice?
3. Would she come over during a snowstorm and shovel you out of your troubles?
4. Showing people how to treat you is acceptable and necessary sometimes.
5. People will give you their all; please return the favor.
6. Be the best friend you can be.
7. Take nothing for granted.

FRIENDSHIP CYCLE #7
The Trunk

"True friendship is when you walk into their house, and your Wi-Fi connects automatically." – Author Unknown

Our friends impact our decisions, influence where we live, eat, and sometimes what we purchase. Our friendships develop from one level to another as the individuals improve themselves. The important thing is that no one woman is an island; we are friends who blossom into a Garden of Life.

Look around you; which one of your friends is still there? This is your friend for life. As mentioned, I have ten friends in this cycle; we are closer than blood sisters. I could call them any time of the day or night. They will take my deepest secret to the grave. Do you have a friend you can trust like this?

THE TRUNK

The Trunk Friendship Cycle friend is the most rewarding. The SOLID FOUNDATION is where all your hard work pays off. This is the most profound relationship you will encounter. Your connection will be priceless, and your bond will be stronger than glue.

This cycle is based on being able to be oneself, being treated equally, and being the best you can be. Friends care for each other and have a mutual understanding; the ability to support each other emotionally is a requirement. Empathy is also especially important; friends know they can be open without fearing judgment. The Trunk empowers women to step up and take charge. No matter who is around, she is authentic in her interactions and doesn't care who sees her at her lowest.

There is nothing fake here—just 100 percent pure cotton, 24-karat gold, a platinum record, titanium steel, and solid rock to the end. There will be no breaking branches, blowing leaves, peeling bark, twisting vine, waterless seeds, or rotten roots; all of that is in the past. There will only be love flowing over. There is no bitterness or drama between you two, although there may be some involving others trying to break you apart. It is not going to happen on your watch, though. This bond will not be easily broken.

The level of respect for each other is immeasurable. You know the foundation is strong, and the friendship will never end. There is no expiration date on a lifetime commitment. Plus, you know you are best friends when she knows your middle name.

Being vulnerable will only bring you two closer. There is no need to keep your guard up in this cycle. You have experienced the worst with each other, and now you can enjoy the fruits of your labor.

Friends who shop, drink, and gossip together stay together forever.

Now, go and enjoy your "forest of friends!"

SAP TIME

You made it! It was a long journey, but you're here now. Connecting with others is what you prayed for. All your hard work, patience, and determination have paid off.

When you truly invest in your relationships like you have by reading this book, God rewards you with amazing lifetime friendships that make your entire life better.

Great friends help you fulfill your purpose in life!

STANDING ON A SOLID FOUNDATION
THE TRUNK FRIENDSHIP CYCLE

1. Thank God for making it to the end and finding a fantastic friend.
2. Believe in yourself; your friend sure does.
3. Life is great at the top. Stay true to yourself.
4. Carry a rope. You will need it to pull each other up from time to time.
5. Your foundation is strong; keep people who try to come between you out of your friendship.
6. Be that "ride or die" friend.
7. Not everyone will find that "diamond in the rough" friend, but you have.

Congratulations!

Practical Ways to Deepen Your Friendships

At different stages of our lives, friends can mean everything to us. Friendships play a significant role in defining who we become. It's a beautiful thing if the parties involved are all fully committed to it. Treasure the people in your life, whether they are here for a reason, a season, or a lifetime, and be thankful for the gifts you received from them.

One of my concluding thoughts is to learn to forgive, speak up, and move on quickly. If you have any issues with your friends, you should be able to be open with them. Little piles of offenses can turn to bitterness, and you have too much to achieve to become a bitter woman.

You need great friends that are straightforward, kind, sympathetic, reasonable, real, and astute. Be that individual first, and you will draw that kind of friend into your life.

These accompanying points will help you improve your 7 Friendship Cycles:

1. **Pick Your Friends Carefully.** I know this is a little strong, but it is the truth. You do not have to be everybody's friend. Connect with individuals who will drive you to develop and improve. They will not dissuade you from your dreams. Pick

friends who inspire and encourage you, not choke or hinder you. Life is a function of choices.

2. **Maintain a Distance from and Don't Attempt to Settle the Majority of Your Friends' Issues.** If they solicit your recommendation and advice, don't hesitate to give it. You may be required to edit a vital email before it is sent. Possibly they are battling some serious issues. Maybe life is taking a toll on them, and they need your help or understanding. Never attempt to squirm your way into your friend's life; this can be counterproductive. Rather, disclose to them how they can be the star of their own life. Afford them the space to process things and make their own decisions.

3. **Be Yourself and Act Naturally.** Be straightforward. No matter what you become, never become fake. You can only attract genuine friendship when *you* are real. More damage is caused by being fake than the good it might appear to offer. Building up a friendship will be hard if somebody cannot acknowledge you for who you are. Do not deny yourself your convictions, qualities, and perspective just to fit in. You will not help anybody.

4. **Embrace Transparency and Sincerity.** Creating correspondence with a woman can require some serious energy—and trust! Ask your friends about what you can do to help them improve their experience. Give whatever it is you have to their improvements. Be sincere and honest always.

5. **Give Compliments.** Don't just be quick to correct; show your friends you appreciate their outstanding qualities. Don't hold back should you spot one quality or two worth

celebrating. A simple "I am proud of you" can work magic. Let your friends see that you value their friendship. Sometimes a handwritten note can be the perfect way to do this. Compliments are one of the easiest and most affordable ways to keep a relationship going. Better yet, show appreciation by taking her to lunch or dinner. It is the thoughtful things that are priceless.

6. **Concede and Apologize.** When you do something wrong, admit it. Figure out how to apologize. Occasionally, your friendship may be disturbed, and all that's needed from you is to honestly say, "I am sorry." It demonstrates that you understand your slip and will ideally not commit a similar error.

7. **Give Up and Let Go.** Did your friend hurt you badly? Have you talked it through? Were expressions of remorse made? If so, let it go and proceed onward! If you don't, you will cling to the transgression, which will hinder the relationship from developing.

8. **Stay Faithful to Your Commitment.** Loyalty is a gift, and it can go a long way. Be supportive, honest, respectful, and trustworthy even during the dark times. Have her back and follow through on commitments.

9. **Communication.** Communicate effectively. This way, no one will be kept in the dark.

10. **It is Time to Tailor Your Schedule and Set Aside Time for Great Fun.** Please go out and accomplish something fun or look at that list of new things you've always wanted to try

and attempt one of them. Having a friend you can hang out with who can relieve your burdens and allow you to feel free while in her company is incredible.

11. **Make Up Your Mind to Be a Team Promoter.** Commit yourself to empowering others. Never speak ill of your friend; instead, promote her and what she does. Confirmation goes far. Your real friends will speak well of you anytime, no matter what.

12. **Keep Your Friend's Privileged Information Private.** As connections develop, it is normal for friends to share personal information. Your friend reveals her secrets to you because she believes you will keep what you know in the strictest confidence. Do not sell out your friends by offering their stories to others. Many relationships have been destroyed over spilled privileged information.

13. **You Should Not Be Afraid to Let Go.** Friendships develop and evolve, and at times they end. You can change a considerable measure in a year. Envision the amount you can change in five years. The individual you were when you met somebody is not the individual you will always be. As humans, when you alter your opinion about things, your friends will do likewise. Infrequently, a companion you have known for a considerable length of time will begin to assume a more significant role in your life. This companion may remain in your life but may have less positive effect and impact on it. That is all right. Should your friend cut you down, harm you, or hold you back, it is reasonable to end such relationships. Sometimes, these relationships ultimately rob us of many good things because we hesitate to let go of them.

A Final Word

Well, I hope you enjoyed this book as much as I enjoyed writing it, even if it took me two decades to finish it. Writing has been my passion since I was a little girl, and I knew I would one day become a published author. I must say, it feels great to accomplish something I have worked so hard on.

It wasn't always easy. I was writing a book about friendships and felt I was losing friends by the minute. Some of my friends didn't realize how much time, determination, and dedication it took me to stay focused on the task ahead. There have been some long nights and days of writing and then rewriting because doubt would sneak in from time to time. In all, I can say this is a product of sacrifice. Even if I had to sacrifice some friendships on the way, it was worth it!

Having healthy friendships means so much to me, and I want to pass this knowledge around, *one friend at a time*. Life is too short for us to keep to ourselves. I believe God put us on this earth to connect with others, and I am not wasting any time.

I have been extremely fortunate to have found my "Trunk friends," Cat, Debra, Ederique, Antoinette, Sharon, LaTeesh, Rosa, Bean, Patrice, and Lisha. I would not change that for anything in this world. I would not be the person I am today without them. I pray you find yours as well.

I want to thank each of you for taking the time out of your busy schedule to read my first book. I know you got a lot out of it, so please purchase my book for your friends because I'm sure they will also benefit from it. Because without your friends, you wouldn't be who you are today. I've always known that true friendship is a big part of life, and it is imperative to keep in contact with others, even if it is only for a short time.

And remember, when you look outside today, stop and enjoy that tree before you. As you form friendships, your one lonely tree will become a *beautiful forest.*

Acknowledgments

To my loving husband—where would I be without you by my side.

To my daughters, Breanna Jackson and Areanna Luckett, I love you all to the moon and back.

To my parents, Jimmy Watson and Leah Felicia Myles, thank you for bringing me into this world and making it all possible. Pat Watson, I'm glad you and my dad found each other. Dorothy Rodgers and Paula Forest, thank you for shaping me into the woman I am today.

To the Beta Readers and Advisors: Donna Lehman, Terri Hart, Linda Jackson, Paula Wheeler, India Smiley, Dorothy Williamson, Christy Debrezeny, and Tanya Hawkins: you have taken my book from awesomeness to magnificent. Thank you!

To my "Trunk" Best Friends: Antoinette Davis, Lisha Johnson Lewis, Ederique Goudia, Sharon Searcy, LaTeesh Claypool, Louise "Bean" Johnson, Carolyn "Cat" Watson, Rosa Baker, Patrice Smith, and Debra Robinson.

I can't forget all of my family and friends, it just too many to list here. You know I hold a special place in my heart for you all.

Special Mentions: to my aunts: Patrick Hamilton, Catherine Miller, Orkrita Hudson, Sharon Tyus, Minnie Lee Etherly, and Mary Robbins. Great-aunts: Jeanette Laws and Sandra Smith. Goddaughters: Sharell and Shanell Searcy, continue to make your parents so proud of you.

Q&A with the Author

1. WHAT IS THE DEFINITION OF FRIENDSHIP?
TL: Well, *Merriam-Webster's* definition is "a relationship between friends." To me, friendship is our lifeline, our journey to happiness. When our friendships are going well, we are happy and healthy, and we want the world to know about it. But when they are not, our health starts to decline, and life as we know it becomes one big blob of bad outcomes.

2. WHY ARE FRIENDSHIPS IMPORTANT?
TL: Studies have shown that we do well when our friendships are good. Friendships are important because everyone wants to be healthy, loved, and appreciated. When our friendships are solid, our stress level is down, our mental health improves, and we make better and more sound decisions. Positive vibes always produce a positive atmosphere where great things are bound to occur.

3. WHY DO A LOT OF FRIENDSHIPS FAIL?
TL: There are a lot of reasons why friendships fail. One is the lack of concern for the feelings of the other. Sometimes, it is always me, me, me, me, and me. At some point, you will need to turn and help someone else and put your feelings aside. Some people are not willing to let others shine. A person cannot be 100 percent right all the time; there are two sides to a coin. For a friendship to work, both parties must give up something and stop looking for something in return. It is just that simple. Be willing to love your friend as yourself.

4. CAN LACK OF FRIENDSHIP AFFECT OUR HEALTH?

TL: There are so many research studies out there that have proved this point. Think back to when a friendship was not going well or when you felt your friends replaced you with another friend. How did you feel? Did you feel sad, angry, or furious? None of these emotions make you feel good inside. When a person is experiencing an adverse emotional reaction, their body will react as well. How else can you explain the headaches, stomach pain, or even breaking out into a rash? Negativity brings negativity back in.

I had a personal experience with a friend with whom I got so close that we were almost inseparable. Then we began to drift apart, and it was as though we were strangers. I later realized that I had been replaced by someone who was her friend first. The pain started as jealousy and faded into feelings of unworthiness. Later on, even as my friend thought there was no reason for me to be mad and we could continue the way we were, it was almost impossible for me because trust was lost. Whenever you have the opportunity for a great relationship with someone, make sure you do not mess it up. Not every friendship is worth losing.

Sources

Aristotle in his Nicomachean Ethics. 2001. Aristotle's Ethics (Stanford Encyclopedia of Philosophy). Plato.stanford.edu/entries/ashingto-ethics/

Benudiz, Kathy Kay. N.d. Friendship quotes. MotivationalDepot.com. docs.google.com/document/d/1iyhpER-pXxHHYYPnv_rjvJyOMCIZ5juGWA6geJAcN3E/edit#heading=h.vy79ial6ztjk

Braun, Ruth Bergen. 2017. Friendship is like a sheltering tree. Mourning Minutes. Suddenlysinglesurvivalguide.com/friendship-sheltering-tree/

Braxton, Toni. 1992. Love Shoulda Brought You Home

Chapman. Garay. 1992. The Five Love Languages. The Secret to Love That Lasts. Northfield Publishing, Chicago.

Chirban, John T., Ph.D., Th.D. 2013. Do your friends double your joys and divide your sorrows? The power of true friendship. Harvard Medical School. Psychologytoday.com/us/blog/alive-inside/201307/do-your-friends-double-your-joys-and-divide-your-sorrows

Coleridge, Samuel Taylor. N.d. Youth and age. Poetryfoundation.org/poems/44000/youth-and-age-56d222ebca145

Degges-White, Suzanne, Ph.D. 2015. Toxic friendships: knowing the rules and dealing with the friends who break them. Northern Illinois University.

Psychologytoday.com/us/blog/lifetime-connections/201503/do-you-need-friendship-cleanse

Degges-White, Suzanne, Ph.D. & Borzumato-Gainey, Christine. 2011. Friends forever: how girls and women forge lasting relationships. Rowman & Littlefield.

Diels, Kelly. 2018. TRUTH: 'You can't be friends with someone who wants your life." Kelly Diels. Kellydiels.com/cant-be-friends-with-someone-who-wants-your-life-oprah/

Djossa, Erica, September 17, 2013, The five stages of friendship. The Love Compass. The-love-compass.com/2013/09/17/the-five-stages-of-friendship/

Ford, Henry. N.d. Henry Ford quotes. Goodreads. Goodreads.com/quotes/34931-my- best-friend-is-The-one-who-brings-out-the

Gracian, Baltasar, Spanish Philosopher. N.d. Quotable quotes. Goodreads.com/quotes/364358-true-friendship-multiplies-the-good-in-life-and-dividesits#:~:text=Strive%20to%20have%20friends%2C%20for,keep %20him%20is%20a%20blessing.%E2%80%9D

Hartwell-Walker, Marie. 2016. Daughters need fathers, too. Psych Central. Retrieved on June 18, 2018, from psychcentral.com/lib/daughters-need-fathers-too

Hill, Napoleon. Napoleon Hill quote. Goodreads. Goodreads.com/quotes/77253- whatever-the-mind-can-conceive-and-believe-it-can-achieve

Jahren, Hope. 2017. Lab girl. Vintage Books. Pg. 30.

Mayo Clinic Staff, nd. Friendships: Enrich your life and improve your health.

Mayoclinic.org/healthy-lifestyle/adult-health/in-depth/friendships/art-20044860

Oakes, Tiffany. (2017). 6 tips on communicating with others. eLearning Best Practices. Elearningindustry.com/communicating-with-others-6-tips

Psychology Today. 2013. How dads shape daughters' Relationships. Psychologytoday.com/us/blog/inside-out/201307/how-dads-shape-daughters-relationships. Kromberg, Jennifer PsyD.

Quotes on seed include. Inside the seed are many trees… Inside You are many kingdoms. bing.com/search?pglt=43&q=seed+quotes&cvid=2bbbeb8baf5b41aab422e2e4407fa5a4&aqs=edge.0.0l9.4625j0j1&FORM=ANNTA1&PC=LCTS

Vanzant, Iyanla, Dr. 2012. Iyanla: fix my life. www.oprah.com/own-iyanla-fix-my-life/iyanlas-reflections-why-women-cant-get-along-video#ixzz5Eq05P4Si

Washington, George. n.d. George Washington quotes. brainyquote.com/quotes/george_washington_132907

Whitaker, Scott. 2011. A Sheltering tree–friendship. Impact for Living. impactforliving.com/2011/05/09/a-sheltering-tree-friendship/

Williamson, Sarah Marie. 2017. 4 kinds of friends you should reconsider. goodreads.com/work/quotes/48295241. University of South Carolina-Aiken. theodysseyonline.com/4-kinds-of-friends-you-should-reconsider

Winfrey, Oprah. n.d. Oprah Winfrey quotes. Goodreads. goodreads.com/quotes/221293-if-Friends-disappoint-you-over-and-over-that-s-in-large

Wohlleben, Peter. 2015. The hidden life of trees: what they feel, how they communicate—discoveries from a secret world. Greystone Books. Vancouver/Berkeley. Pgs. 15, 17, 18, 25, 26, 49, 61, 63

Merriam-Webster. Friendship Definition & Meaning. Merriam-webster.com/dictionary/friendship

The 7 Friendship Cycles Profile Quiz

The 7 Friendship Cycles Profile will give you clear insight and a thorough analysis of your view on your current friendships. It will guide you to your primary friendship cycle, show you how to connect on a deeper level, and explain what your friend means to you. Some would give anything to make their relationships work but expect friendships to thrive without any assisting factors. If you appreciate your friends and value your friendships, you should do what it takes to ensure their growth.

There are thirty-six paired statements below. From each pair, select the statement that best describes your friend. The profile will not take long, so don't rush the process. Allow about ten to fifteen minutes to get through the thirty-six paired statements. After you have chosen from each pair, tally your results. The last page of the profile will help you interpret your results.

Write your friend's name here: _____:
[Fill in the blank] YOUR FRIEND...

1	appears approachable and friendly	A
	doesn't keep your secrets	B
2	pays you compliments	B
	wants all the attention to be focused on her	C
3	speaks badly of you	D
	will defend your character and honor, even when you don't	G
4	will share the spotlight but doesn't want to	E
	will not let you give up	B
5	shows judgment toward you and your decisions	C
	is slowly moving the friendship in the right direction	A
6	is a strong-willed person	F
	will be there for you no matter what	B
7	respects your views and has respect for herself	B
	never has anything positive to say	D
8	has no respect for others	E
	is dependable	F
9	adds value to the relationship	F
	is a loyal, honest, and truthful friend	G

THE 7 FRIENDSHIP CYCLES

10	open to meeting new people	A
	will cover for you	B

11	doesn't make time to hang out together	C
	knows her worth and yours too	G

12	never judges you	F
	doesn't speak up on your behalf	C

13	thinks her issues are more important than yours	D
	will share details about her life	A

14	will lie to make herself look better	C
	appreciates the good things in life	A

15	opens up the more you get to know her	E
	tries to outperform you	C

16	doesn't worry about what others think	B
	drains your energy, motivation, and spirit	D

17	wants to see people grow	A
	can be flaky at times	E

18	says one thing but does the opposite	C
	wants to see you blossom	F

19	gets mad at you often	C
	appreciates the good things in life	A
20	is not afraid to let you into her life	B
	clicked with you instantly	A
21	never asks how you are doing	D
	wants nothing but the best for you	F
22	uses your friendship to control you (manipulative)	D
	looks for the positive in everything	F
23	is comfortable around you	A
	offers a strong foundation	G
24	has your best interests at heart	C
	will be there to push you to your full potential	G
25	only talks about herself	D
	gives great advice	B
26	can be closed off and defensive	E
	never speaks ill of you	G
27	is not dependable at times	E
	guides you in the right direction	G

28	is your rock	G
	shows you different sides (negative or positive)	E
29	listens attentively without judgment	A
	never shuts up about her problems	D
30	listens to your problems attentively	B
	doesn't care about hurting your feelings	D
31	calls often but doesn't add any substance to the call	E
	roots for you to succeed	F
32	is always in your corner	G
	doesn't get along with your other friends	C
33	tries to be someone she's not	E
	has your back no matter what's going on	F
34	never gives up on you	F
	pretends to like you	E
35	shows jealous tendencies	D
	focuses on growing the friendship	A
36	is happy to hear from you	B
	can be trusted with your life	G

Add up all your circled answers and record the number of responses to your statement here.

A Seed	B Leaf	C Branch	D Vine	E Bark	F Root	G Trunk

INTERPRETING YOUR PROFILE SCORE

There are no right or wrong answers here; these are just pointers to clarify your cycle and help you realize some things. The highest score indicates your friendship cycle. Do not worry if you have two high scores; it means you are between the two cycles, which is not uncommon.

THE OTHER FRIENDSHIP CYCLES

Now, have your friend take the profile quiz with you. It will benefit you to know what cycle you fall in, according to your friend. It will be all right if you scored high in the Branch cycle and your friend scored high in the Bark cycle. This means your friendship is headed in the right direction. You are still learning about each other.

Now, if you scored high in the Bark cycle and she scored high in the Vine cycle, the friendship doesn't necessarily need to end. You will need to communicate so you can fix any misunderstandings.

Remember to discuss your results with your friends. This will allow the friendship to grow.

Notes

Author Bio

Tina Luckett is from Van Buren Township, Michigan. She is a U.S. Army veteran with a heart of gold and a natural desire to experience life to its fullest.

Tina earned her Master of Science degree in Administration-Leadership from Central Michigan University. With a career spanning a decade, Tina has accumulated a lifetime of experiences allowing her to write her novels.

Tina is married to her best friend of over 34 years. The couple has two adult daughters they raised with the same decency and thoughtfulness as they treat others.

Tina has been a lifelong writer. Her first book was fiction, but her heart lies with nonfiction. While The Suite Tea Society, Boss Moves Series books continue gaining popularity, she hopes to bring readers the same levels of happiness as she feels today.

Follow Tina on Social Media:

Website: www.TinaLuckett.com
Email: TinaLuckett7@gmail.com
IG: @Tina_Luckett7
FB: @Lucketteer

Review Ask

Love this book? Don't forget to leave a review!
Every review matter, and it matters a *lot!*
Head over to Amazon or wherever you purchased
this book to leave an honest review for me.
I thank you endlessly.

www.ingramcontent.com/pod-product-compliance
Lightning Source LLC
Chambersburg PA
CBHW071006080526
44587CB00015B/2368